Scien
All Around

Elizabeth Tarski

Rigby®

A Harcourt Achieve Imprint

www.Rigby.com
1-800-531-5015

Winter

Spring

Summer

Fall

Science All Around

A Journal of
My Year in Colorado

Summer in the Rocky Mountains

Summer

I can't believe it! We get to move across the country and live in the Colorado Rocky Mountains for one whole year!

I'm so excited about this, I've decided to keep a journal. That way I can remember everything that happens. I love that Mom and Dad are scientists because we're always getting to do fun things. Once we spent a summer living on an island while Mom and Dad studied dolphins. This time we're going to live in a cabin in the middle of the mountains while Mom and Dad study the weather. I love going to school with my friends in Florida, and I'm sure I'll miss them, but I think Colorado will be a lot of fun, too.

Look how far across the country we're going!

Since I want to be a scientist like my parents, I'm going to keep a journal of all the things I observe while we're living in Colorado. Mom and Dad are always saying that science is all around us, and this log will help me understand how that's true. They've promised that we can have at least one science adventure each month.

This is our home in Colorado!

Date: June 20, 2006
Time: 6:30 p.m.

How Temperatures Are Different in
Florida and Colorado

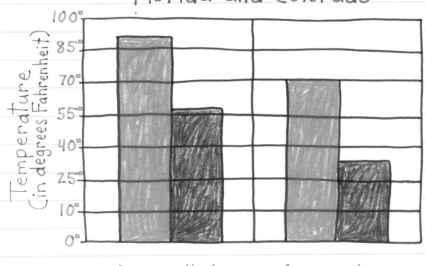

Temperature (in degrees Fahrenheit)

100°
85°
70°
55°
40°
25°
10°
0°

Average High   Average Low

The Month of June

■ Florida
■ Colorado

We'll move in 2 days and until then, I'm going to spend my time learning everything I can about my new home. I already know the temperature will be really different, but I wonder how cold it will get in the winter?

July 14

We've been here for 3 weeks now, and I've really gotten to see what things are like up in the mountains. The other day, we went on a hike for our first science adventure, and there was snow on the top of the mountain we climbed! I got to throw a snowball in the middle of July, which was great, but then I asked Mom and Dad what any of this had to do with science.

Isn't the view great?

They pointed out that even though we had left the house in jeans and T-shirts, we were now wearing jackets. Then they explained that this is science. The top of the mountain is so much higher than our house (which is at the bottom of a lot of mountains) that the air is a lot colder. Science is all around!

Even when we're not on top of a mountain playing with snow, the elevation in Colorado is very different than in Florida. Colorado has the highest elevation of any state in the U.S.

Mount Elbert is the tallest mountain in Colorado. Its elevation is 14,433 feet, and it takes 8 hours to climb!

Elevation is just a measure of how much higher a place is than the ocean, and the elevation of a place helps determine what the temperature is. The temperature drops about 3.5 degrees every time you go up 1,000 feet. That's why there isn't any snow on the ground by my house, but there is snow at the top of this mountain.

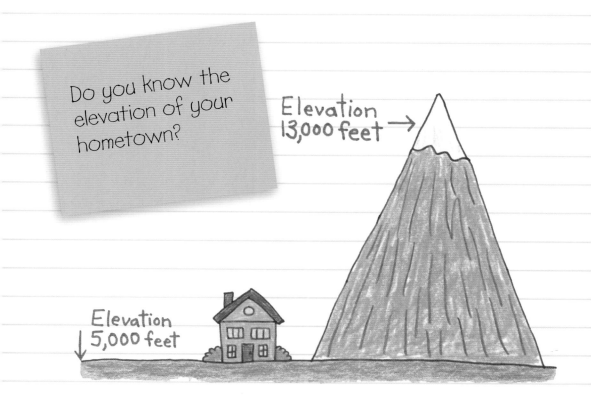

Do you know the elevation of your hometown?

Elevation 13,000 feet →

Elevation 5,000 feet

Date: July 14, 2006
Time: 5:00 p.m.

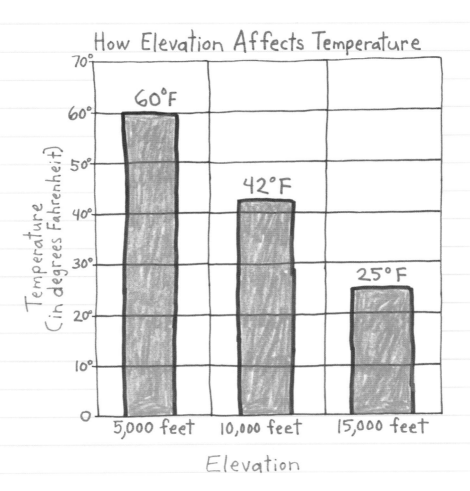

How Elevation Affects Temperature

Temperature goes down as elevation goes up.

August 19

   Lately it's been raining more. Mom and Dad said the
rain tells the animals it's about to get cold. We've been
watching a family of squirrels outside our kitchen window.
They're gathering more food each day, and they're so funny.
They constantly look around and twitch their noses, as if
someone is following them, planning to steal all their nuts
before the winter comes.

This squirrel thinks we're going to steal its food.

We have a pond in our backyard that just keeps getting bigger because of all the rain. As soon as Mom said there were lots of living things in the pond water, I knew we were going to have another science adventure.

Today we went and took a sample of the water in the pond. Then I got to look at it under Mom and Dad's microscope! I wonder what the water in Florida looks like under a microscope?

There are a lot of different tiny animals living in our pond!

Fall

September's Science Adventure

Sept. 27

The weather is awful, which means that today was
the perfect day to do the experiment we had planned. We
walked outside to learn about the weather. It's not raining,
and it's not snowing. It's sleeting, which means ice is falling
from the sky. When a cloud releases precipitation, it's always
either liquid or solid (rain or snow), but sleet happens when
snowflakes melt on the way down and then meet cold air all
of a sudden. They re-freeze, but instead of becoming white
and sparkly, they just become needle-like ice.

How Sleet Forms

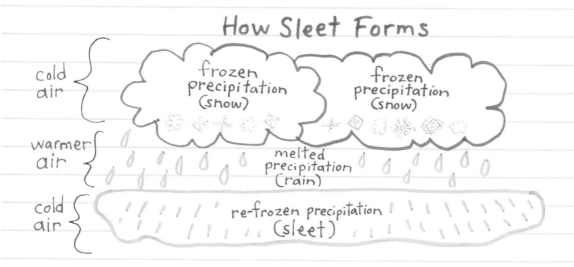

cold
air

frozen
precipitation
(snow)

frozen
precipitation
(snow)

warmer
air

melted
precipitation
(rain)

cold
air

re-frozen precipitation
(sleet)

I really enjoy learning all these new things while I'm here, but it's a little frustrating at my new school. I'm not doing too well in science, which is crazy because I love it! Mom and Dad say that because science is all around, I just need to keep observing everything that I can and I will improve in class.

The leaves on the trees are all changing colors now, and I especially love the bright yellow Aspen leaves. Mom helped me collect a bunch of leaves to save. First, I had to press them dry. Next, Mom ironed the leaves between two pieces of wax paper. Now I can keep them in my journal!

Aspen leaf

October's Science Adventure   Oct. 29

It's snowing today! This is the first time I've ever seen it snow, and it's amazing! When I went to sleep last night, everything was dead, brown, and boring, but when I woke up this morning, the world was white and soft.

Look at all the snow!

So far I've built a snowman and had a snowball fight. I can't wait to go snowshoeing and snow skiing, but it needs to snow a lot more before I can do either of those.

I like that snow falls so quietly. Rain and sleet are noisy, but snow just drifts to the ground and makes everything look nice, like a winter wonderland.

This is the snowman I built!

I sort of expected snow to feel like sand, because they look a little bit alike in pictures, but I was wrong. Snow and sand have almost nothing in common. Sand is grainy and usually warm. Snow is wet, even when it hasn't melted, and is never, ever warm. It's not as soft and comfortable as it looks, either. No one would want to lie down on the snow and take a nap. When I went outside, I had on three layers of clothes, and by the time I came back in, they were all soaking wet from my science adventure!

Making shapes in the snow is fun!

Colorado snow is cold and wet. You need a lot more clothes if you want to lie in the snow.

The beaches in Florida are covered in sand that is warm, grainy, and gritty.

November's Science Adventure   Nov. 8

Last month the snow didn't stay very long. The temperature would get too warm after a few days, and the leaves on the trees and plants would lose their white dusting of snow and go back to brown. Usually the trees had icicles hanging from them each morning and water dripping off of them each afternoon.

These icicles were outside my window.

Now that the snow stays all the time, I've discovered that I love sledding—it's so much fun. You just jump on your sled and fly down the hill. Even better, it became this month's science adventure!

We've been having sled races all week, and I won a couple of times, even though the kids around here have been sledding for years and I haven't. I won because I know the secret: Science is all around! The steeper the hill is, the faster you go, but you can also control the sled by moving your body one way or the other. I think it's really cool that science has been helping me win sled races.

My sled!

Winter

December's Science Adventure   Dec. 27

The pond whose water we saw under a microscope this summer is now completely frozen! Mom, Dad, and I agreed that as soon as there was 5 inches of solid ice on the pond, I could try out ice skating. As part of our science adventure, we've been using a chisel to make holes in the ice each week to check how thick the ice is. When the ice was finally thick enough, we threw a bucket of water over the pond. When I got up the next morning, the water from the bucket had frozen, and I had a smooth, clean surface to try to skate on!

Our frozen pond

When a pond has 5 inches of solid ice on top of it, it's strong enough to support one person. To support a hockey game or anything heavy (like a snow blower or a snowmobile), the ice needs to be at least 6 inches deep.

Date: December 27, 2006
Time: 5:30 p.m.

How Thick the Ice Is on the Pond

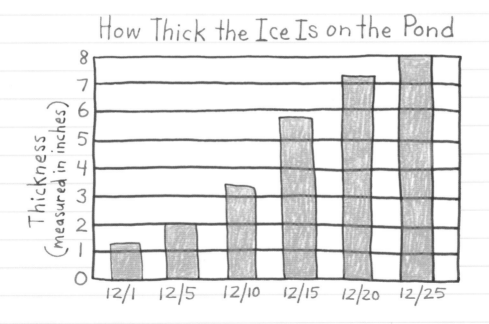

Unfortunately, I did not look anything like the people you see ice skating on TV—I fell down all the time! Also, ice is so slippery that it's hard to get up once you do fall. If I ever make it to the Olympics, it will not be as a championship skater. I was glad our pond is so small, because no one else was there to see me skate so badly during my science adventure!

Now that I'm living in Colorado, I've come to respect hockey players more! All my friends here love hockey, so I've been learning about all the different teams and the rules of the game. My friends in Florida don't know much about hockey, so I've been writing to them about it.

My skates!

Having grown up in Florida, I still have trouble believing that the ice I was skating on this afternoon is the same water I swam in this past summer. It's fascinating. If I wasn't already planning on using this journal as my science fair project this spring, I would probably do a whole project on ice. Maybe I'll do a project on ice for the science fair next year.

The ice is thick enough to skate on.

January's Science Adventure Jan. 11

Lately I've been learning how to ski. It's really hard, but I think it's fun, too. The other day I fell a lot, so I was covered in snow. When we got home, Mom decided to make this month's science adventure about snowflakes. She called me into the science lab and showed me microscopic images of different kinds of snowflakes. It was amazing! There's so much to see. Some snowflakes look alike, but really, they're all different and unique. Also, some fit into certain categories, and others are just "irregular" snowflakes, which form any way they want. It's hard to believe that they're all just frozen water when they're each so beautiful.

How to Make a Snowflake

I wanted to send all my friends back home some of the beautiful snowflakes here, but since they would melt, I made paper copies. I folded over a piece of paper lots and lots of times, and then made different cuts in the folded paper.

These snowflakes look like
the perfect snowflakes
you see on postcards.

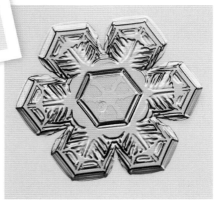

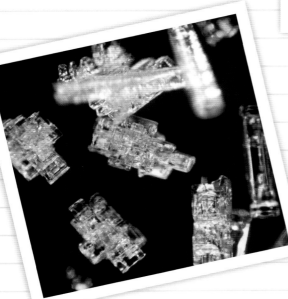

Most snowflakes
actually look like this.

27

February's Science Adventure   Feb. 28

Last weekend we went snowshoeing at Rocky Mountain National Park for our science adventure. January and February are the best times to go snowshoeing, because before now there wasn't enough snow, and next month the snow might get really icy. Snowshoeing works best on fluffy, powder-like snow. I only know all of this because a park ranger told us while he led us along several paths in the park. To snowshoe, you have to learn a whole new way to walk. You have to take really big steps and constantly stop to shake snow off the big shoes. It's kind of like wearing paddles on your feet.

It's strange to walk in snowshoes.

I wore snowshoes like this. Snowshoes have been used for more than 6,000 years!

When you're wearing snowshoes, you can go places you can't normally go, because your weight is spread out over a large surface, instead of being focused in just one small place. When your weight is spread out, you don't fall through the snow and get wet up to your knees. To explain this, the ranger took off his snowshoes and walked a few feet—all of a sudden he was up to his chest in snow! Then, he put the shoes back on and walked all over the same area without ever sinking more than a few feet. Now that is science in action!

Date: February 28, 2006
Time: 6:15 p.m.

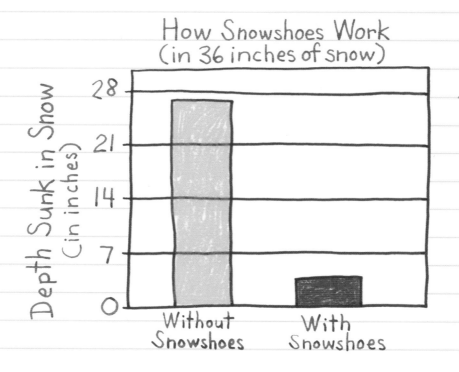

How Snowshoes Work
(in 36 inches of snow)

This is the data I collected when I tried the snowshoe experiment. But snowshoeing is hard to graph. There are lots of different kinds of snowshoes, and people that weigh more sink farther into the snow. My dad sank a lot farther than I did!

This is the log cabin we stayed in.

After snowshoeing our way through the park, we spent the night. Since it's so cold, we didn't stay in a tent like we would have at home; instead, we stayed in a log cabin. The cabin was nothing like being at home, because we didn't have much furniture and we had to use sleeping bags, but it was at least 20 degrees warmer inside the cabin than it was outside.

Spring

March's Science Adventure

For Spring Break this year, we left the cold, icy Rocky Mountains in Colorado and went to visit the Grand Canyon in Arizona. It was great! The canyon itself is the biggest thing I've ever seen. And the red rock is so pretty. We got to go hiking and camping.

The most amazing thing about the whole trip was when I finally understood that this huge, beautiful area was created by water, wind, and ice! It took years and years, but eventually erosion carved away at the different kinds of rock until the canyon was formed. By gradually breaking down the soil and rock, water came down the Colorado River and pushed open an entire, huge canyon of space.

Isn't this view amazing?

This is Bright Angel Trail. It was originally a
Native American trail. We spent half a day on
this hike and took lots of pictures.

April's Science Adventure   April 15

I am ready for spring! I love snow, but now I want sunshine. The flowers are ready for sun, as well. They are in bloom now.

The snow is melting, and it's messy! People up here call it "sludge." It's soupy and mixed with mud. Sludge is not pretty at all.

I do like watching the rivers gradually get bigger and bigger. The more snow that melts, the more water there is! All the dry creekbeds have water in them again. All that water rushing down from the mountains makes a roaring noise that doesn't sound like anything I've ever heard before.

Spring in the mountains is amazing!

In Colorado the rivers and streams have much more water rushing through them in the spring than during any other time of year. This is because all the snow that was coating the mountains all winter starts to melt.

The other day I was wondering where all the melted snow, ice, and sludge will end up, so Mom and Dad made my question into our next science adventure. We looked at some streams and rivers. When we got home, they showed me a big map and explained that the water I like to watch rushing past will keep on going until it gets to a bigger body of water.

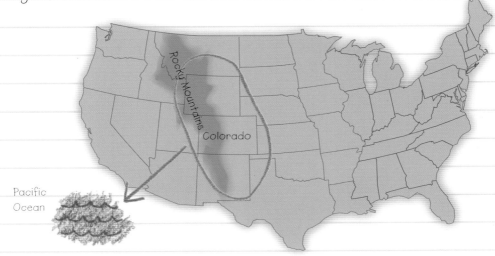

Almost all of the water in Colorado ends up in the Pacific Ocean!

May's Science Adventure

Since it's finally warm again during the day, we usually eat lunch by the pond. The picnics are always fun, and yesterday we had our last science adventure in Colorado. Dad had me find two pebbles that were the same size. Then he had me find a big leaf. I put one of the pebbles on the leaf and it sailed around the pond. Then I tried to put the other pebble on the water. No surprise, it sunk. But when Dad asked me why, I couldn't answer. Why, if both pebbles were the same weight, did the one on the leaf float?

This pebble has a little boat.

Dad explained that it's because, again, science is all around! The pebble on the leaf floated because of buoyancy. That just means the more surface something covers, the more likely it is to float. It's the same reason I could walk across three feet of snow with snowshoes on. The snowshoe covered more ground than my foot would have, just like the leaf covered more water than the pebble did.

Buoyancy is why a ship can carry tons of heavy things and float, even though if you threw those same heavy things off the ship, they would sink to the bottom of the ocean!

I can't believe this ship floats!

Eureka!

A famous Greek scientist named Archimedes discovered buoyancy. We'll never know exactly how, but legend says that one day, Archimedes sat down in his too-full bathtub and some of the water spilled out. Suddenly, he realized that weight and water were connected. He was so excited by this discovery that he jumped out of the bathtub, yelling "Eureka!" That means "I've found it!" in Greek.

How It All Came Together   May 18

Now that I'm finished with this journal, I will turn it in to my teacher, so that she can enter it in the science fair. Even if I don't win first place, I feel like a real scientist now. The best part of my year in Colorado is being able to explain to anyone I meet that science is all around.

Guess what. . . I won first place in the science fair! I'm so happy, especially because I was having so much trouble in my science class at first. But keeping this journal helped me a lot. I'm on my way to becoming a real scientist!